In the Garden of His Presence

Veronica G. Burnette

In the Garden of His Presence

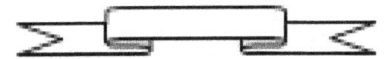

Ready Writer Publishing

Copyright

Unless indicated, all scriptural references are taken directly from The King James Holy Bible.

All rights reserved and protected under International Copyright Laws. Any contents within this book including its cover may not be reproduced in whole or in part without the express written permission or consent of the author except in the case of brief quotations embodied in news articles, newsletters and/or reviews.

Copyright © 2016 – by Veronica G. Burnette
All Rights Reserved.

Published by:
Ready Writer Publishing
United States of America

ISBN: 0-9743773-7-6

Veronica G. Burnette
www.veronicaburnette.com

NOTICE

The information within this book is not by any means inclusive. The intent is to provide practical examples of personal growth, development and spiritual intimacy with God as experienced by the author.

Dedication

I dedicate this to everyone who encourages me through their passionate pursuit for intimacy with the Father. There is no better place than our Father's lap. I am thankful for a journey filled with growth, wisdom and insight obtained by resting in God's presence. I am also thankful for every opportunity to impart and teach others how to grow their relationship. It is a pleasure to entice individuals to plunge deeper and experience times of refreshing through spending time in *The Garden of His Presence*.

Acknowledgments

I give thanks to God for my Mother, Dora Burnette, who is one of my greatest supporters. You've taught me more than you know. I love you to the moon and back.

*To my entire family who are too numerous to mention because if I did, it would read like Matthews 1:1-18. I love and thank **ALL** of you for supporting the vision, plan and purposes God has for my life.*

*To my sister and BFF, Brenda Tyson Tate, for being a consistent role model and encourager to **"do this thing called life"**. No matter what task I embark upon, you inspire and motivate by putting me in remembrance of God's Word. I've learned a great deal by watching your relationship with Father. You are more than a friend. I call you FAMILY!*

Thank you to all who believe in the vision God has given me. You have prayed and spoken prophetically into my life. As iron sharpens iron, you have been a tool in the Master's hand to fine tune areas within my life. I am extremely grateful to each of you near and far. I pray your life be enriched and the blessings of God continually overtake you. May the tangible evidence of His abundant grace be magnified throughout every area of your lives.

Last, but certainly not least, I thank my son who motivates me to be a more effective role model; who encourages me to never stop dreaming on this journey of **Making Life Happen**.

Life is Good!

Content

Preface 11

Where I Find Rest 15

In The Beginning 19

More Than This 29

Knowing God as Father 47

Date Nights 59

Preparing a Meeting Place 73

Memorial Stones 83

The Process of Excavation 97

Final Thoughts 117

About the Author 123

Preface

I am extremely passionate about my relationship with Father God. This is my answer to self-care. God is my source, everything else is simply a resource to what I need in order to make life happen. I have come to understand many things about life. It is full of personal perceptions that shape our reality. Our personal realities are rooted in our life experiences. Unfortunately, many of these life experiences blind us from truth and keep us locked into cycles of dysfunction.

It was not until I opened my heart to Jesus and began developing a personal relationship with Him that my eyes were opened to the truth and the reality of grace. I have come to know the authenticity of love through intimate fellowship with the Holy Spirit. I now have the ability to love and embrace love beyond my fears.

Because God's way of doing things is perfect, He teaches me how to view life and live it from His perspective. The more I know of Him, the more I want to know. It is an increasing desire that drives me to know Him better. It is this same desire that fuels my passion to help others in their pursuit to know Him better as well.

While lying on the floor one afternoon as I often do during worship, I heard Father say "True Image". I said *yes Lord, that's my name*. Veronica in Latin means True Image of Christ. He said *No, that's who you are. That is your ministry*. It was at that moment I understood the purpose behind my passion.

Nothing about God or getting to know Him is hard. It is our lack of understanding that causes our life and heart to become hard. In my journey to know Him, I have come to understand the message of His love and the gospel of grace is quite simplistic. Likewise, my goal is to provide simple truths and examples of how to grow and develop through intimacy with Father. Since much of my ministry focus is relational development, I am consistently asked and given platform opportunities to share regarding my relational pursuit. However, there seems to never be enough time to give due diligence to this topic.

For this reason, I was inspired to write this book as a way of providing a window's glimpse into a few of my experiences.

Jesus said unto him, if thou wilt be perfect, go and sell that thou hast, and give to the poor, and thou shalt have treasure in heaven: and come and follow me. But when the young man heard that saying, he went away sorrowful: for he had great possessions. (Matthew 19:21-22).

If you are more concerned with anything other than the heart of God through intimacy, my prayer is, by the time you reach the end of this book, your heart will be changed. I pray for the object of your affections to be developed into greater levels of understanding to know God as Father. According to Jeremiah 29:11, I pray for your heart to become stirred with a greater passion to search out His thoughts, plans and desires for you. I wish above all things that you will come to know Him outside the boundaries of being Jehovah-Jireh. He is so much more than your provider. May you come to enjoy abundant life and experience your full inheritance as a kingdom citizen.

There is so much in store for you. God's desire is for you to live in abundance. It is my desire and expressed purpose to help make that happen by any means necessary. I encourage you right there where you are to keep your head up and never stop dreaming. It is never too late to set new goals and make your dreams your reality. It all begins with a decision. You alone hold the power to make that decision. Your life matters. Make it count!

Where I Find Rest

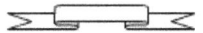

As deep calls to deep, beyond the surface, my heart longs to know; beyond what I see, beyond what I've been told. Your book is an autobiography, a simple glimpse of who You truly are, which is not sufficient enough to contain the totality of you by far. So, I go to the secret place to discover the part of You that seems to be concealed. I call to You with worship. I call to you with praise because it is in Your presence where the mysteries of You are revealed.

In this place, I find solutions for everything I need. Refuge from life's storms and troubled waters are made calm; a place of comfort protected by your strength and peace. The fragrance of your smile and the calming touch of *your voice; it's not a place of struggle or a mandated chore. It's a **get to** opportunity, a pleasure; yes, necessary choice.*

Worthy of the sacrifice of whatever it takes to get to this place; filled to momentary capacity only to inevitably be met with a new hunger, a greater thirst for another taste. Never completely satisfied desiring to further understand, it turns into passionate pursuit for more wisdom and knowledge beyond the tangible substance released from your hand. It becomes a matter of knowing your heart, your mind I crave so much. It's you I crave more than the tangible stuff. Although I've come to appreciate your provision that comes from this place, I'd rather spend time getting to know you better because everything else I need has already been provided and appropriately funneled through grace.

Your heart welcomes the weary and all who have been wounded by life and all its mistakes. In your presence is restoration, strength, a fortress for escape, streams of mercy and pools of healing flowing freely from heaven's gate. There are many alternatives, places to disappear, that are no more than temporary fixes. But, in the garden of your presence, hurting hearts find rest in comfort and forgiveness.

A place of sanctuary you are and spending time here is always a pleasure. In the garden of your presence are hidden mysteries and such beautiful treasures. What's so amazing about the mysteries found in this place? They have been hidden for us and access is never denied to anyone who is thirsty and in need of a resting place.

~ **Veronica** ~

Deeper Lord, DEEPER where your presence drowns out everything except the sounds of glory's rest; caressed in the arms of GRACE and LOVING righteousness.

In The Beginning

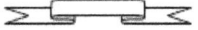

We were not born of this earth, which is why we are constantly searching for something beyond our human existence. There is an internal instinct in every one of us seeking to know our origin. This search for satisfaction and fulfillment is a part of being human. It is an innate longing we all have. It is a call of the heart causing us to search for what some would refer to as both purpose and fulfillment. It drives us to explore, to experiment, and to be fascinated, thereby trying to fill the void. However, this is often met with momentary and fleeting satisfaction. Until the void is filled with what that space was meant for, there will be a continuous search for purpose throughout this earthly existence.

There is a place or origin outside of the natural realm where the supernatural beckons us. It is a place where spirit meets Spirit. It is a place where time ceases to exist, mysteries are hidden and answers to life's purposes are revealed. It is a place where God is saying **COME**. It is a place where desire is saturated, soothed, fulfilled and fortified. It is this very place where information becomes revelation and the lens through which we view life becomes clear. It is in this place with God that secrets are revealed and wounded hearts are healed. This is a place I've come to know as the garden of God's presence.

Keep thy heart with all diligence; for out of it are the issues of life. (Proverbs 4:23).

A garden is a place of growth, production and reproduction. In the garden you will always find some type of growth taking place. The way you tend the garden will determine the type of harvest and how much of it will be produced. You may not consider yourself to be a gardener, but everyone has a garden to tend. It is the garden of your heart. The heart is our life line and whatever we plant and allow to grow there will manifest throughout our lives.

A good man out of the good treasure of his heart bringeth forth that which is good; and an evil man out of the evil treasure of his heart bringeth forth that which is evil: for of the abundance of the heart his mouth speaketh. (Luke 6:45)

If you want to know what is in a person's heart, you only need to listen to their conversation. The abundance or the overflow of what is in a person's heart can be determined by what they are consistently speaking. Everything about our human condition, whether it's mental, emotional or physical, is affected by the condition of our hearts. That's why scripture teaches us to guard and protect it with all diligence.

And the LORD God took the man, and put him into the Garden of Eden to dress it and to keep it. (Genesis 2:15).

In the book of Genesis, God placed Adam in the garden and gave him the responsibility to dress and keep it. Therefore, it became man's responsibility to maintain what God provided. As with our individual gardens, it is our responsibility to do the same. No one is going to care for your garden the way you do. Ask any farmer. They will tell you they take pride in watching their harvest grow. They take pride in seeing the harvest and the fruit of their labor. Keep in mind, the type of seed you plant will be the harvest you receive.

In the beginning was Eden, which in Hebrew (גַן, *Gan*) means Garden of God. It was a place of purity, beauty, peace, comfort and prosperity. It was a place of abundance and never ending growth. It was in this place mankind met with God. Not only did God meet them, He communed with them regularly. Eden encompassed everything mankind needed that pertained to life and sustaining their existence. The Garden was a place of life, production and reproduction. Everything God made was good. There was no corruption or anything beyond the righteousness and purity of God, until evil entered. God gave man the blueprint and the commands to follow. He never stripped them of their ability and the right to make decisions. While in the midst of evil, mankind still had a choice between right and wrong.

> *Be not deceived; God is not mocked: for whatsoever a man soweth, that shall he also reap. (Galatians 6:7)*

There are consequences and repercussion, both good and bad for every decision we make. It is human nature to blame others for our decisions. This appears to have been established when Eve made the choice to do what God commanded them not to do. His instructions to them was *do not* eat from the tree of knowledge of good and evil. Since this rule was not followed, the consequence was sin resulting in separation from the place of presence. Sin brought death and separation from God, but Jesus restored life and fellowship with God. It is through the sacrifice of Jesus we now have the right to approach the throne of grace with confidence (Hebrews 4:16), knowing we have received mercy and grace for everything we need. This is the good news of the Gospel of Jesus Christ. The Garden has been restored and there you will find everything you need, in the place of God's presence.

Within each of us God has placed a desire for connectedness and intimacy. God created us with relationship in mind. His design is for us to have relationship with both Him and each other. To say you do not desire to be close to anyone or can do without affection is to deny God's creative reasoning. Denying the need for intimacy or rejecting it stems from a place of pain and brokenness. Intimacy is a place of privilege, which has to be allowed. However, if you do not value its importance, it will never become important enough for you to pursue. God woos us because He has a longing to commune with us too. He desires to be with us, more so than we desire to be with Him. Consider that denying the gift of intimacy with God is to deny Him the privilege of being with you.

> *And when Simon saw that through laying on of the apostles' hands the Holy Ghost was given, he offered them money, Saying, Give me also this power, that on whomsoever I lay hands, he may receive the Holy Ghost. But Peter said unto him, your money perish with you, because you have thought that the gift of God may be purchased with money. You have neither part nor lot in this matter: for your heart is not right in the sight of God. (Acts 8:18-22)*

We all have passion and our passions are identified by the object of our pursuit. Many of us are like Simon. We become short-sighted and get caught up in obtaining gifts and talents. We then fall short when it comes to pursuing God, seeking to know His heart, and living a life that manifests His desires above our own. Scripture teaches us gifts and callings are without repentance (Romans 11:29). We don't need to ask God to give us those. They are irrevocable and were given to you from the foundation of time. We simply need to ask Him to help us understand what they are. There is so much time wasted praying for what we have already been given. This is why it is important to read the word of God and understand our Kingdom inheritance.

> *Lay not up for yourselves treasures upon earth, where moth and rust doth corrupt, and where thieves break through and steal: But lay up for yourselves treasures in heaven, where neither moth nor rust doth corrupt, and where thieves do not break through nor steal: For where your treasure is, there will your heart be also. (Matthew 6:19-21)*

We have become inundated with obtaining substance making it very easy to lose focus on what is really important. By today's standards, success is determined by popularity and how much money and possessions we own. All of the stuff and things we spend our lives accumulating will pass away, but your love for God will remain. It is a combination of love mixed with deep levels of pursuit that will determine your level of intimacy. More than anything, I believe our relationship with God is our greatest asset.

> *I am thy shield, and thy exceeding great reward. (Genesis 15:1b)*

God allowed me to know some time ago that our seeking Him is often limited to substance. We have been taught to pray during times of crisis or when we need something. Don't be misled. There is nothing wrong with seeking Him for things we need. However, we should never allow our prayers to be this limited. I recently read this quote, "If the only time you pray is when you're in trouble, you're already in trouble." According to scripture, we are to always seek God and His way of doing things. This means to consistently purse His nature and striving to be like Him. I believe when we pursue His heart, He will show us how to manage our need.

> *for your heavenly Father knoweth that ye have need of all these things. But seek ye first the kingdom of God, and his righteousness; and all these things shall be added unto you. (Matthew 6:32b - 33)*

We are to seek first the Kingdom of God and His righteousness, which means God's way of doing things. He promises everything else will be provided. I believe when our main focus becomes knowing God's heart things will change. You will notice your list of priorities and prayer requests will be different. When we have a greater understanding of His desire versus our desires, tangible possessions will become less important.

The garden is a dwelling place. A dwelling place is where one lives. It is a resting place. May you find rest and realize the answer to everything you need is found *In the Garden of His Presence.*

*God knows how to get our attention.
Sometimes, our holy frustrations are no
more than a phone call from heaven.*

~ ~ ~

More Than This

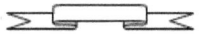

Verily I say unto you, except ye be converted, and become as little children, ye shall not enter into the kingdom of heaven. (Matthew 18:3)

I remember my first experience at church somewhere around the age of four or five. I recall sitting in Sunday school at the little AME church on those hard wooden pews. This is where I first began hearing stories about Jesus and how important He would be to my life. I could not wait to meet Him. To my disappointment, I waited and waited but never got to meet Him because I wasn't properly introduced. So, I continued to attend church every Sunday because, after all, this was the proper thing to do. I made friends and enjoyed the activities. This was especially true of Vacation Bible School because arts and crafts were a major to do. Every year we would have Easter egg hunts either in the park or somewhere on the church grounds. We would end the day with a huge community picnic that included all sorts of games and activities. To a child, this made going to church quite fun, which gave me something to which I could look forward. Church became a second home, as we spent quite a bit of time there. These were my humble beginnings; but, can I tell you how I met this Jesus I had heard so much about? I said my prayers as I was instructed. Unfortunately, I still failed to have an understanding regarding the concept of Jesus, His life, His ministry or the importance of His death. I only remember being introduced to the moral principles of being a good person. Along with that, two were certain. Jesus died to save us and I needed to be a member of a church in order to avoid going to hell.

> *And said, Verily I say unto you, except ye be converted, and become as little children, ye shall not enter into the kingdom of heaven. (Luke 18:17)*

The faith of a child mixed with their imagination is quite phenomenal. Seeing things from their perspective is simple and innocent. Children have a tendency to believe the impossible. This is why scripture teaches us to come to Jesus as a child because they believe what you tell them. Therefore, it is extremely important for us to sow good seed into their gardens. They have such untainted views of the world around them. Unfortunately, as we witness on a daily basis, they grow up and become touched by a stringent belief system. The values of the world's system coupled with the cares of this life have a phenomenal impact in ways that are sometimes unimaginable.

As a child, my view of God was one of total distance because of the saying He *is a God who sits high and looks low*. In my childish thinking, I envisioned God as someone who was plastered on a throne with a book in His hand writing down everything we did, highlighting the wrong. Now, with Jesus being at the right hand of the Father, I imagined Him looking over God's shoulder and agreeing with what was being written based on Jesus' encounters with us. He would not only record the events of our lives, but He was also recording our prayers. I kept hearing about this *Book of Life* as a book God would regularly read to make judgments against us. I imagined this book to have so many eraser marks and white out marks in it because of my repenting and asking for salvation almost daily. I became afraid of God and wanted to avoid His wrath. In order to keep my name written in the book, I had to become someone He approved of and someone who would never disappoint him. I believed I needed all the brownie points I could get in order to make it into heaven.

As you can see from my description, my imagery of God was someone who looked like the Greek god Zeus, standing in heaven with lightning rods ready to strike us for the wrong we do. Because of this, I would repent every night just in case He decided to strike me during my sleep on a particular day when I really misbehaved. With everything being recorded, it was my understanding once I made it to heaven, Father would take out His book. Like Santa Claus' naughty or nice list, we would discuss everything I had done, said and asked for during times of prayer. I would finally get all of my questions answered. He would then explain to me all the mysteries of life.

My belief in angels was as equally imaginative. Their job was to gather and bring messages from heaven like the one in the Christmas story.

> *And the angel said unto them, Fear not: for, behold, I bring you good tidings of great joy, which shall be to all people. For unto you is*

born this day in the city of David a Saviour, which is Christ the Lord. And this shall be a sign unto you; ye shall find the babe wrapped in swaddling clothes, lying in a manger. And suddenly there was with the angel a multitude of the heavenly host praising God, and saying, Glory to God in the highest, and on earth peace, good will toward men. And it came to pass, as the angels were gone away from them into heaven, the shepherds said one to another, Let us now go even unto Bethlehem, and see this thing which is come to pass, which the Lord hath made known unto us. (Luke 2:10-15).

I understood their sole purpose was to fight the evil angels that fell with satan and keep them from harming people. However, there was a stipulation to their protection. They were specifically assigned to those who had confessed salvation and given their hearts to Jesus. Again, children believe what they hear and what they are taught. I was taught to say my prayers every night because God was listening for them. Even though I knew the only time I would actually have a conversation with Him was when I got to heaven, this did not stop me from storing up plenty to talk about for when I finally get to see Him.

There was one prayer I remember quite vividly, and I prayed it consistently. *Lord, I want to help you help people. I want to see into the future and tell people which way to go and what to do to avoid danger.* This became my earnest desire. I kept praying this prayer for a number of years despite my limited knowledge. Even as a child, I believed we were put here for reasons beyond our comprehension. So, I continued to pray and believe for the impossible. As you can probably tell by now, I had a vivid imagination. I actually believed the stories I would read in the Bible, learn about in Sunday school and see on the movie screen. Surely, if the Lord gave supernatural powers back then, He would still do it for a select few even now. So, I continued to pray and believe: *Lord I want the ability to see into the future and help you help people. I want to show them which way to go so they can have a good life.* One thing I love about God and that is He is intentional and extremely strategic. I realize now, those prayers were not in vain. I see how they have and will continue to manifest in my life.

Another vivid memory that invoked an additional request from heaven was a movie entitled *Resurrection* starring Ellen Burstyn. She was miraculously given the power to heal after being involved in an accident. She was able to lay her hands on sick people and they would be healed. One particular scene, which was the most powerful scene in the movie, in my opinion, left a lasting impression on me. In this scene, Ellen went through her regular routine of trying to heal, but this particular time it was not working. She repositioned herself to lie beside the woman in order to heal her. The deformity of the woman was transferred to Ellen. The woman was completely healed, but Ellen suffered a few days because of it. The thought of being able to heal the world's suffering became fascinatingly real to me. I was convinced I too needed this gift.

I believe the reason this movie was so impactful to me was that this woman was just another ordinary Jane Doe. She was someone who did not believe in Jesus Christ. At least this was my assumption since Jesus was never mentioned. One would think God would have been given some sort of credit since He, the originator would be the one to grant such a gift. Keep in mind, I was a child and was thinking like a child. Based on the seeds of knowledge I had concerning the spiritual gift of healing and the working of miracles, there were only a selected few to which God granted these gifts. I wanted to be one of them. If I was to be instrumental in helping God to help His people, surely, I would need them. So, I began incorporating this request into my prayers.

Everything is movie screen big when you are young. When I prayed, I expected things to unfold just like it did in the movies. The innocence of youth is such a beautiful thing. I expected any day and at any moment, I would miraculously have this power bestowed upon me. Until then, I would continue to pray. I don't quite remember the exact moment, day or hour I gave up, but I did. I do remember thinking maybe I was not one of the handpicked special ones. Thoughts are seeds that become planted in the heart and produced through our actions.

> *Above all else, guard your heart, for everything you do flows from it. (Proverbs 4:23).*

I'm sure it was somewhere around this time I began to believe God really doesn't answer prayers like we are taught. Here entered the seed of doubt. However, there was enough faith already planted that had taken root for me to hold on to, leaving some glimmer of hope. In my heart I knew there was something more to this thing of being a Christian. So, I continued to pray and believe as I struggled with doubt. God knows how to get our attention. Sometimes our frustrations are nothing more than His phone calls.

Fast forwarding to the day I saw what I now know as the presence of the Holy Spirit. I was approximately 14 or 15 years old at this time. I remember a certain woman who would sit on the front row pew at the little Missionary Baptist Church I attended for many years. At a certain point in the service during singing and worship, something would happen to her that was a little different from the responses of anyone else. It appeared as if something took hold of her. It was not frightening, just different. I perceived it to be something supernatural but was unsure. I became quite intrigued. Because of that, my curiosity got the better of me. I wanted to understand it better. The problem was, I did not understand what it was or how to pray and ask God for it. My petition to God became *Lord, whatever she has, I would like to experience it*. Coupled with my previous petitions, I prayed these prayers fervently. Each week I expected an experience, but to no avail. As it is written, the carnal mind cannot understand the things of the Spirit (1 Corinthians 2:14). I understand now the problem was my ignorance of God and not understanding the person of the Holy Spirit. This was another time of disappointment, resulting in additional seedlings of doubt. However, this did not stop me from going to church. I was still under the impression that church attendance was required to make it into heaven. Out of routine and ritual, church attendance became quite boring. My attendance became sporadic until one day I noticed I had stopped going altogether.

During a period of about ten years, I would continue going to church searching. Perhaps maybe I would have an encounter, or find something I might have missed before. Unfortunately, each time I left disappointed.

And he said unto them, Follow me, and I will make you fishers of men. (Matthew 4:19)

One Thursday evening, on April 3, 1997, my life was forever changed. This was during a period of emotional turmoil in my life. I met a young woman who was very instrumental in my decision to give church one more try. She had an excitement and enthusiasm about going to Bible study I had not experienced before. It was the bait God used to hook me into trying it one more time. Here again, curiosity seemed to work in my favor. What was it that made her so excited about going to church? I pondered, maybe the thing I missed would be found in a different place of worship.

What could it hurt? The next day, I called a friend and asked if she would mind if I attended church with her. Of course she was overjoyed. It was on an unforgettable Thursday evening when I had an encounter with the Holy Spirit.

There were certain doctrinal beliefs that could have kept me from receiving the blessing God intended for me. I was raised Missionary Baptist, but this was a Full Gospel ministry. Women did not preach where I came from, but this pastor was a woman. I was raised not to speak in tongues, but the people in this church spoke in tongues. None of these things mattered, because my emotional state was very unstable. I knew I needed something and I was ready for a change. I had what I refer to as a *woman at the well* experience. It was during the evening altar call that I had a profound encounter with God. It was the spark I needed to reignite my pursuit of him. The pastor prayed and spoke things to me only God knew. I had not shared these things about my life with anyone. I suddenly realized how real God is and His presence was not far off. I also became intrigued to know what else He had to say concerning me. It was an extreme breakthrough and an eye opening experience.

After leaving church I felt refreshed and full of hope. I could not wait to get back to church the next Sunday. I was very excited to be experiencing something new and different. It seemed as if every message the pastor preached was being solely directed at me, and it was good. This woman did not know me or anything about my life. So, how could it be? I had not experienced preaching with such conviction as this in my previous experience of attending church. I was having encounters with the Holy Spirit and the *rhema* (spoken) word was convicting my heart unto righteousness. It was not condemning; it was corrective guidance like a skillful surgeon. My desire to understand drew me in and created a bigger thirst to understand God even more. It was at this point my journey into intimacy began.

Now that I knew God was speaking, the focus became how I could get Him to speak to me. I did not have much experience in the area of prayer. It was my thought that prayer was an acquired talent. In order to get God to respond, one had to be an expert. I now know this is far from being true. God responds to our simplest request. Nonetheless, I felt inadequate and uncomfortable when it came to praying. Unfortunately, this is a major barrier for so many when it comes to spending time with God.

God knows how to get our attention. He knows what we need even when we don't. He appeals to our individualities. He knew I felt inadequate about praying verbally. Therefore, I believe He used my ability to express myself through writing to communicate my heart to him. Instead of praying in the traditional sense, I began journaling and writing my prayers in the form of *Dear Jesus* letters. I would journal at least once a day, which was usually at night when everything was quiet. At night was when I had opportunity to relax and think after a busy day. I would flood the pages with everything on my heart. At the end of each letter, I would end with an *Amen* and meditate until falling asleep. Periodically, I would pray the words on the page aloud. This helped me gain confidence to pray outwardly without reading what I had written. This continued to develop over time.

Journaling is an excellent way to spend quiet time with God. If it is not a part of your intimate time, you may want to consider adding it. It is not a requirement, but due to its many benefits, I would highly recommend it. I have found it to be very therapeutic and extremely helpful when looking back and realizing how my relationship has matured over the years. I no longer use it as a primary tool of communication, but I still use it to process my thoughts. I also have a dream journal I use periodically. This is especially helpful when I have dreams I know to be prophetic in nature. I may not understand them at the moment they happen, but will often look at them later and discover the meaning. Journaling also helps me remember details that fade from memory over a period of time. Hindsight has clearer vision. Being able to look back at your dreams will sometimes allow you to have clarity and gain insight into what God wants you to know.

Another area of feeling inadequate for many is reading and studying the Bible. You've heard it said before or even have said it yourself, *when I read the Bible, I don't understand it.* I felt this way as well. However, being one who typically does not back away from a challenge, I kept reading and focused on what I could understand. This was the New Testament. Unless I was directed to other areas of the Bible during Bible studies or Sunday school, I would not venture into the Old Testament.

> *"but the Advocate, the Holy Spirit, whom the Father will send in my name, will teach you*

all things and will remind you of everything I have said to you". (John 14:26)

But whosoever drinketh of the water that I shall give him shall never thirst; but the water that I shall give him shall be in him a well of water springing up into everlasting life. (John 4:14)

Even though I did not understand all of what I was reading, I continued making regular deposits because I believed the Holy Spirit would help me understand it. God's word is a living and active well of wisdom we can draw from and mature. So, I continued to read it daily whether I understood it or not. I enjoyed discovering what was written to the point of reading into the wee hours of the morning. There really is nothing new under the sun (Ecclesiastes 1:9). The same things that happened in biblical times are some of the same occurrences happening now, which make scriptures eternally applicable.

One of my first recognizable encounters with God caused me to seek out the mysteries written in scripture, particularly the parables. One night in April 1997, I had a dream where I heard God tell me to read Matthew 13 verse 8 and 18. I immediately woke up after hearing this and began questioning myself whether it was verse 8 or 18. I had yet to venture into the book of Matthew.

> *but other fell into good ground, and brought forth fruit, some an hundredfold, some sixtyfold, some thirtyfold. (verse 8)*

I did not understand why He would have me to read this because I did not understand it. I was confused. I began thinking, maybe it was verse 18 I am supposed to read.

> *Hear ye therefore the parable of the sower. (verse 18)*

You can imagine my excitement when I realized I had indeed had an encounter with God. This also dispelled any doubt I had about not being able to hear God. Not only did He give me instruction, but He explained those instructions even before I asked. The Holy Spirit is a wonderful teacher. This encounter sparked a question and answer period between me and God. When I read something I did not understand, I would pose a question and proceed to write that question in my journal. Sometimes, not every time, He would send the answer in a dream by way of scripture. Then there were other times, He would send a familiar personality to speak to me in my dreams, such as my pastor or some other spiritual leader in my life. Dreams were one of the tools God used in training me to hear His voice. Some dreams are more impactful than others and imprinted in memory. One dream in particular was when a gentleman approached me and said *thank you for the letters*. When I woke up the next morning, I realized it was Jesus who was thanking me for the *Dear Jesus* letters. At the time of this encounter, I had been journaling for quite some time. It was also His way of answering my unspoken curiosity of whether or not He was even reading or hearing my heart through those letters. God is a loving Father, and the more time we spend in the secret place of His presence, the more we get to know him.

God is a Father who will never forsake His children. He wants us to run to him, not from him.

~ ~ ~

Knowing God as Father

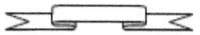

Jesus saith unto him, have I been so long time with you, and yet hast thou not known me, Philip? He that hath seen me hath seen the Father (John 14:9)

The Hebrew word for father is Abba which means creator, preserver, guardian, protector. One of the most prominent figures in a child's life is a parent, specifically the father. He is someone who has an extreme and influential presence. A child's experiences of how to relate to others is frequently molded by their relationship with their parent(s). From a child's perspective, a father represents love, strength, protector, healer and teacher, to name a few. Fathers have the power to shape the emotional, psychological and spiritual health of their children. His influence impacts His children's self-esteem, self-image and confidence. The type of relationship a father has with his child also influences the child's ideas and opinions about God's role in their life.

We are creatures of habit and are shaped by our environments. It is a well-known fact that we cannot give what we do not possess. This also holds true as it relates to our emotional well-being. The type of environment a child is reared in often manifests itself in their behavior, when relating to others. If they are cultivated in a nurturing and loving environment, they learn to love and expect to be loved. When they are brought up in an environment of turmoil, dysfunction will in many cases become their reality. When the father is absent emotionally and/or physically, it leaves a void. Their children may search for love and validation in the wrong places. Unfortunately, the child grows into adulthood undeveloped and emotionally off balanced. This result then becomes an identity crisis. Attempts are made to fill this void, perhaps through inappropriate behavior, unhealthy relationships and all sorts of ungodly things.

It is quite common to find individuals who do not have healthy relationships with their earthly fathers, who are also apprehensive in their approach to God. They lack confidence when it comes to His love for them. This has caused many to avoid, fear or shy away, because the role of a good father was not modeled for them in the earth.

I am the youngest of seven brothers and sisters. I lost my father at the young age of six years old. Where the memories stop, my colorful imagination began. As you can probably imagine, there were plenty of times I found myself in situations that required parental guidance, specifically a father's input. My missing him was extremely difficult. When it came to fixing things, physically, emotionally and financially, I had no provider. When my heart was hurt and I needed someone to hold my hand, I had no protector. When I needed advice, I had no counselor. Most of all, when I needed a hug, my comforter was gone. This was the void of him being absent from my life. The memories I have are limited. Much of what I know of him was revealed to me by other family members and friends. Because of these stories, I filled in the blank spaces by imagining what life would have been like had he lived to watch me grow up.

> *Finally, brethren, whatsoever things are true, whatsoever things are honest,*

> *whatsoever things are just, whatsoever things are pure, whatsoever things are lovely, whatsoever things are of good report; if there be any virtue, and if there be any praise, think on these things. (Philippians 4:8)*

The imagination is a powerful thing, which is why we are encouraged to keep our minds on things that are righteous. As stated in the previous chapter, I am a dreamer. Even now, my dreams are quite vibrant, action packed and displayed in living color. For many years after my father's passing, I dreamed of him frequently. In many of these dreams, my father appeared to have aged as I grew older. Another thing about these dreams, they seemed to have a theme and most of the time ended the same. There would be a scene where I would discover he was still alive and well; after which I would confront him about leaving us. On many occasions, not all of them, I would become angry during these confrontations. The next morning I would wake up feeling sad, angry and sometimes emotionally drained. Because of the dreams frequency, after a while, I simply shrugged them off and explained them away as just another insignificant part of sleep. The day finally arrived in June of 1997 when I would finally understand their significance.

> *I will not leave you as orphans; I will come to you. (John 14:18)*

It was during a time of prayer I heard God speak these words *I am your Father, I never left you.* In an instant, it seemed as if the series of dreams I was having about finding my father finally made perfect sense. The fact of finding him still alive was very significant. Even the details of the angry confrontations were significant and this revelation would later bring about great deliverance from some emotional struggles. What God was trying to get me to understand was despite the absence of an earthly father, I have a heavenly Father who is still alive. All I had to do was simply recognize and receive Him as Father. Scripture teaches, God will never leave us nor forsake us (Deuteronomy 13:8). That was the beginning of my journey of embracing God as Father.

After finally understanding the meaning behind the dreams, I could finally move on, so I thought. Approximately two years later I began having these same dreams once again. It was the same scenario of finding my father alive and becoming angry with him about leaving. Why now, why again Lord? For what purpose, other than satan's attempt to torment me, would I possibly be having these dreams again? This was my question to God. I would quickly come to know this had nothing to do with evil or any demon. It was God's way of getting my attention and helping me to further understand a place of hindrance in our relationship. There were additional things He needed me to understand about my life.

In order to move past an issue, you must first confront the problem. The years of emotional scars resulting from my father's passing were obviously issues God wanted me to deal with. Becoming whole meant I would have to recognize and deal with the painful emotions that were keeping me from receiving God's love. What God was about to show me was quite surprising. He allowed me to know the anger I was carrying was not only because of an absentee father; in fact, the majority of my anger was directed at Him. Of course, I was in denial and tried to shrug it off. It was my belief that to be angry with God was a sin and to sin meant certain death. With the help of the Holy Spirit, I now understand this to be another instance where scripture is taken out of context.

God helped me realize and face my issues. He began speaking to me and said *you are angry* with me. My response to Him was *No! I'm not angry with you. I can't be angry at you, you're GOD!* He responded, *I know I'm God, but you need to know you're angry so you can be healed. Do you want to know why you are angry*, He asked. *You are angry with me because you feel I took your father away from you.* Intellectually, it made no sense to be angry about something beyond someone's control such as an illness related death. My fathers' death was not in his control and logically, it made no sense to be angry, right? As I sat back, I began to ponder on what God was saying to me. Yes, there were plenty of times I would ponder the question of why my father had to die, but I had never correlated any emotional instability as a result of being angry with God. I thought about it for a few seconds. Then I came to the realization which resulted in a river flow of tears brought on by the pinned up emotions. With a loud outburst I yelled, *YES! I am angry with you. You could have cured my daddy and kept him here with me. YES, I am very angry at you.* After a bucket of tears, I realized God's desire was not to harm me, but bring me to a place of wholeness. I began to recognize the negative attitude and emotions I had displayed over the years. The feelings and emotions were not limited to anger, but also included bitterness, abandonment and rejection, to name a few. God went on to share with me the difference between reverence and fear. He said *I want you to reverence me, not be so afraid that you can't come to me.* After this encounter, I became increasingly aware of God's desire and love for me. I was no longer afraid to envision myself approaching Him beyond kneeling at His feet. I could now see myself holding His hand and laying my head in His lap.

> *God is not a man, that he should lie; neither the son of man, that he should repent: hath he said, and shall he not do it or hath he spoken, and shall he not make it good? (Number 23:19)*

God's love for us is not like mankind's love for one another. His love is unconditional and not based on our performance. Scripture teaches us to reverence the Lord, but there is a major difference between reverential fear and fright. Many are possessed with a dreadful fear of God. This fear is a result of being taught to view Him as a stern judge of sinners rather than one who has reconciled us to a loving Father. We tend to avoid what we fear. If we are afraid of God, we will avoid him. God's design and desire is to have intimacy with mankind.

Our primary goal is to increase in wisdom and understanding as we continuously develop our relationship with him. If you find yourself struggling to connect with God, take the time to reflect on your relationship with your earthly father or the lack thereof. It is very likely you are wrestling with mental and emotional strongholds that are causing an arrested development in your emotions toward God. In order for you to progress beyond where you are, these strongholds must be identified and eradicated with the help of the Holy Spirit and renewing the way you think. Suppressed emotions do not happen overnight and the heart becomes calcified over time, which then manifests in many ways. Breaking these strongholds is strategically simple. Sitting in God's presence allows the Holy Spirit to minister and reveal to you every unfortified area.

> *The LORD will perfect* that which *concerneth me: thy mercy, O LORD,* endureth *forever: forsake not the works of thine own hands. (Psalm 138:8)*

The love God has for you extends far beyond the cross. Even now He broods over you like a hen broods over her chicks. He is concerned about every aspect of your life down to the smallest details. What you may consider insignificant, God considers significant. He is your Father, why would He not be concerned? Your net worth is priceless to God. Jesus would not have died for a worthless cause.

> *Are not five sparrows sold for two pennies? Yet not one of them is forgotten by God. Indeed, the very hairs of your head are all numbered. Don't be afraid; you are worth more than many sparrows. (Luke 12:6-7 NIV)*

If God is concerned enough to know how many hairs are on your head why would He not be concerned about everything else? God wants you whole. So, first thing, be willing to admit there is a problem; otherwise, you will remain in denial. He already knows. Confession is opening your heart, which is your way of giving Him what you cannot handle.

> *Come unto me, all ye that labour and are heavy laden and I will give you rest. (Matthew 11:28)*

The comforter is waiting, beckoning you with open arms. Sitting with Him on a regular basis allows the Holy Spirit to help you identify what you cannot see on your own. Once these unfortified places have been brought to your attention, it is totally up to you to change your mindset and get in agreement with what He says concerning you. God wants to perfect (mature) you. This is all a part of the excavation process, which will be discussed in another chapter. Once your vision of God changes, you will begin to see Him differently and approach Him with greater confidence.

> *For we have not an high priest which cannot be touched with the feeling of our infirmities; but was in all points tempted like as we are, yet without sin. Let us then approach God's throne of grace with confidence, so that we may receive mercy and find grace to help us in our time of need. (Hebrew 4:16-17)*

God knows about all you have been through, even the things you have yet to encounter. Remember, Jesus was the word made flesh and experienced every human emotion. He relates to humanity and wants to fortify you for success in all things. He is a GOOD Father who is concerned about His children. You are precious to Him. Make it your goal to get close and personal so you may know Him more intimately as Father.

In order to know God, it is important to make spending time with Him a priority.

~ ~ ~

Date Nights

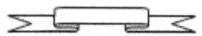

Thou that dwellest in the gardens, the companions hearken to thy voice: cause me to hear it. (Song of Solomon 8:13)

Getting to know you, getting to know all about you; getting to like you, getting to hope you like me too are lyrics to a song by Julia Andrews from the movie entitled *The King and I*. Some relationships are surface, while others are quite intimate. It is a choice as to what type of relationship you will have. Both parties have to be in agreement with that decision. If only one is pursuant while the other is lackadaisical, the relationship will never become intimate beyond a surface level. Intimacy requires an invitation and permission to enter; without which intimacy can and will never happen.

If you were to go to the vital records department in the city where I was born, you would be able to discover pertinent, but limited information about me. You would learn the date and time of my birth, gender, nationality, the names of my parents, etc. Other people can tell you about their experiences and what they know of me. However, in order to know me beyond secondhand information, you would have to take the initiative to know me personally. I would have to fill in the blanks and tell you who I am beyond what is written in public record or the limited information gathered from outside sources. There is a saying, "believe none of what you hear and only half of what you see." The meaning behind this saying is, you can't believe everything you see and hear if you are not involved personally to ask for clarification. I have learned to never make any decision based on limited information. What is the alternative? Go straight to the source.

How does one get to know a person? You must spend time with them; not just any time, but quality time. Quality and quantity determines the level of impact of intimacy. The level of trust that one has will also determine the level of intimacy you allow. They will not be able to see past a certain point. Intimacy (into-me-see), is a place beyond physical and emotional barriers.

Relationships are not established and developed overnight. Intimacy requires time.

In developing a relationship with God, as we discuss throughout this book, it is important to make spending time with Him a priority. This may require you scheduling allotted times in order to meet this demand. When we think about the word relationship, it implies some sort of bond with one another. Spending time with each other is necessary to solidify the bond. Any relationship that does not have commitment within the equation will not flourish or last very long. Commitment and communication are two areas where most relationships fall short. In the hustle and bustle of today's microwave society, finding time to do much of anything requires work. This is partly due to lifestyle demands and the advancement in technology. Although technology provides great modern conveniences, it is diminishing our ability to effectively communicate on a personal level. Before text messaging was made available, if we wanted to make contact with someone, we would have to pay them a visit or pick up the phone and make a person-to-person call. Remember the times you would hold those long conversations with family and friends sometimes lasting several hours? Technology has allowed these personal touches to be replaced with instant messaging, video chats, picture grams, emojis, or some other form of a nonverbal communicating apparatus. This should not be a replacement for spending personal, one-on-one time together. Allow technology to remain within proper boundaries, specifically when it comes to spending quality time with loved ones. Outside of emergencies, the use of technological devices should remain at a minimum.

Technology has also given us a way of escape and a way to hide and not deal with people. But with God, it will never be a substitute. God wants good old fashioned face-to-face time. He wants up close and personal intimate fellowship. As I reflect back to the year of 1997, I continue to recognize how much it was a year of extreme transition. My desire to know God not only became a priority, but again, it became my passion. Good or bad, everyone has passion for something. Whatever you are passionate about is recognized by your pursuit. When you love or are in love with someone, you do whatever is necessary to get to know them and build a relationship. You pursue them, which includes setting aside time to make them a part of your world. You will make it a habit to please that individual and keep them happy. Basically, what you are doing is making them a priority. Why should getting to know God be any different? Why should we not pursue God with the same intensity, if not more? In light of this, I decided God should not have to play second fiddle to anyone. My effort was to give God my undivided attention. I decided I would date God. This may sound a little peculiar, but this was my intimate journey and how Friday evening date nights with God began.

When I consider how much attention I had given to other things and people, there was no other choice but to make date nights a regular occurrence. I chose to spend one evening a week without compromise and without outside interferences. You might be asking yourself, how does one date God? What does it even look like? To me it looked the same way it would if I were to invite a gentleman over for the evening. I would avail myself just as much, as God deserves nothing less. To me this meant having a clean, quiet, non-disturbing and inviting atmosphere, with **inviting** being the operative word. At the time, my son was quite young, and it took some ingenuity to find time for myself. Parenting comes with daily responsibilities that take up much of your day. By the end of a nine hour work day I was often physically and emotionally drained. There were after school activities, cooking, cleaning and whatever else that required my attention made this appointed time quite intentional.

> *After he had dismissed them, he went up on a mountainside by himself to pray. When evening came, he was there alone. (Matthew 14:23)*

> *And in the morning, rising up a great while before day, he went out, and departed into a solitary place, and there prayed. (Mark 1:35)*

> *One of those days Jesus went out to a mountainside to pray, and spent the night praying to God. (Luke 6:12)*

> *And he withdrew himself into the wilderness, and prayed. (John 5:16)*

As shown in the above scriptures, there were times Jesus had to get by himself to worship, meditate, pray and simply be alone with Father. Jesus being our model, we should recognize the importance and the necessity of alone time to process, gather our thoughts and simply be alone. There were also times Jesus would call His disciples away from the crowd to teach them. From time to time, we too are called away from the noise of the day. It is an act of consecrating ourselves, which puts us in a position to hear from heaven more clearly.

> *But when you fast, put oil on your head and wash your face, so that it will not be obvious to others that you are fasting, but only to your Father, who is unseen; and your Father, who sees what is done in secret, will reward you. (Matthew 6:17-18)*

Scripture does not say **if** you fast. It states **when** you fast. Fasting is another important ingredient used to strengthen your ability to hear as you develop your relationship with Father. Fasting teaches us to have discipline and self-control. As with anything, this also requires commitment.

Commitment is another thing that begins with a decision. Once you have made a decision to do something, it will take time and endurance to get it done. One thing about God, there will not always be instant gratification as we have become so accustom to through modern conveniences. Scheduling designated time will help keep you committed. I focused on how I would correlate this within my intimate setting. It all began with a simple invitation, a cry of my heart. I asked Him to show me how I could get to know Him better. I felt this meeting place should not only be comfortable for the Holy Spirit, but it had to be an environment where I could still away both mentally and physically from the routine of day-to-day activities. We will discuss the meeting place in more detail in the next chapter. For me, my meeting place with Him would and should not be just any place, because He is not just anyone. I was preparing to meet the King, and with that, I believe the ambiance of this place is important. This place happened to be the front room area of my home. The room where a guest would be invited into upon entering the front door, especially a guest you don't know all that well. Normally, one would typically get to know a person before giving them access to the rest of their house. This was during the time I was getting to know God. However, God desires more than an invitation. He wants access to the whole house (all of you), and is seeking to abide permanently. Nonetheless, He is a gentleman who allows us to set the pace of the relationship. It seemed quite logical to begin there.

Once I found the ideal location our date nights began. I invited Him to come in and make himself comfortable in my spiritual home (heart) as I became comfortable entertaining Him in my natural environment. Metaphorically speaking, that is where many believers remain. They never allow God beyond the periphery of their internal affairs. They are either not interested in taking their relationship any further or simply not taught how to grow deeper. This is something I hope will be rectified by sharing with you my experiences.

One of the greatest attributes of the Holy Spirit is being a revealer of truth. Knowing this, I began asking Him to show me the things He was not pleased with in order to make it a conducive environment comfortable enough for Him to dwell. This would require rearranging some things. The environment of course, refers to ones emotions, personality, thoughts and anything else in need of change. Rearrangement involves putting things in proper alignment and getting rid of old, familiar and unfruitful things that have been around for quite some time. It is a time of cleaning and decluttering. For example, we keep old furniture in our natural house sometime because of sentimental reasons. We know it's old. It is no longer comfortable and needs new upholstery, but we hang on to it because it has become a familiar fixture in the house. Our thought processes often become this way. We become unfruitful, nonproductive and stagnated yet hold on to them because these ways are familiar to us. This is referred to as becoming set in our ways. We are either fearful of change, refuse to change or do not understand how to make change happen; becoming stuck in methodological systems and patterns that become difficult to break.

> But Jesus beheld them, and said unto them, With men this is impossible; but with God all things are possible. (Matthew 19:26)

Habits may be hard to break, but not difficult. You cannot change what you cannot see or identify as being a problem. It is with the help of the Holy Spirit hidden places are identified, habits are broken and fear is eradicated. Once you know what needs to be uprooted and thrown away, the process of excavation can begin.

Dating relationships will develop and grow through levels, with falling in LOVE being the ultimate goal. The more time you spend with the one you are dating, the more your heart becomes attached to them. My gratitude and admiration for Father began to grow stronger during these Friday evenings so much so, I began looking forward to them. My week would be full of anticipation for those Friday evenings. Like a giddy school girl during the courtship phase of our relationship, I expressed my desire for Him through poems and love songs. As we sat quietly together throughout the evenings, a journal of these poetic writings began to emerge. I would sing, worship and many nights dance for Him. Words cannot adequately express our moments together. It was not enough to just tell Him I loved him; I wanted to do so much more to show him. It was my heart's desire to hear Him smile. To know I was the cause of those smiles made our encounters so much more intimate.

Another example of being in a relationship is like learning to dance with a partner. You both have to find your rhythm. At some point in the dating process, things will begin to surface that would not otherwise be a problem when you are alone. You are forced to deal with relationship blockers consisting of negative emotions and what is triggering those emotions. Being single means not having to deal with such things because you are self-absorbed. Being self-absorbed in this sense is not a bad thing; it simply means you have not been challenged to see from someone else's relational perspective.

> *let us throw off everything that hinders and the sin that so easily entangles. (Hebrews 12:1b)*

Stumbling and bumbling during the dance will happen. It is all a part of the learning the rhythm. Everything in life has a rhythm and a flow, even relationships. When the rhythm is off, the flow is disturbed. In learning to jive with God, there were things impeding the flow and troubling the steps to our dance. These things needed to be corrected if we were to move forward. Of course some steps in our dance were more difficult to learn than others and took more time to learn. But eventually, I began learning His rhythm and how to align with His desires.

I was once blind, but now I see (John 9:25).

Scriptures began to come alive and prophetic words I had put on the shelf began to make sense. Agreement is a powerful tool. When we submit our will to get in agreement with Father's plan, our minds become clear to see what we were unable to see or understand before.

As you continue to learn God's ways and grow into deeper levels of intimacy with him, you will constantly identify areas requiring alignment to maintain a rhythmic flow. There will be times He will show you infractions that are causing problems. The good news is, He waits patiently for you to come to understand what and why He brought it to your attention. He is not showing you these things to harm you in any way. His purpose for revealing is for the purpose of healing. Relationships are an equal partnership. You have a responsibility to do your part by getting in agreement and make adjustments when and wherever necessary.

> *Even so faith, if it hath not works, is dead, being alone. Yea, a man may say, Thou hast faith, and I have works: shew me thy faith without thy works, and I will shew thee my faith by my works. (James 2:17-18)*

I've heard it said that *talk is cheap, but proof is action*. It's not enough to tell God you love him. Take every opportunity to show your love through the process of change.

Peace and tranquility is maintained when you cultivate your atmosphere with worship.
~ ~ ~

Preparing a Meeting Place

When you think about an intimate setting, what comes to mind? I think about a clutter free atmosphere, particularly as it relates to a physical location. I think of a place to get away, gather my thoughts, meditate and escape. It is a place where distractions cease to exist and a place of purpose. I think of a meeting place to be with Father. I refer to this place as a private sanctuary.

I am reminded of the *Holy of Holies* and what that atmosphere must have been like. It was a place where the priest entered for the sole purpose of communing with God. They had to leave the outer court of distractions, pass through the inner court and prepare themselves before entering into this place. Although we are no longer required to go through these physical rituals, it is still a good practice to set aside time and have a place to meditate, pray and simply be still with God. Is a designated meeting place required to have a relationship with God? The answer is no, but it's extremely beneficial. Think of it this way, God loves you enough to prepare a place for you (John 14:3). Why should we not give Him the same love, care and attention? My intimacy journey with God began when I decided to set aside a place and a regular time to meet with Him. Because of the profound impact it had on my life, I will continue this practice and encourage others to use this technique in their growth and development process. When you take the time to establish a meeting place with God, you are being intentional in your pursuit.

Governing your atmosphere is also important. When choosing this special place, look for an intimate setting, perhaps a room or area where there is little to no traffic. This way, you can remain undisturbed for periods of time. In my intimate place, I maintain a constant flow of worship music to saturate the atmosphere with peace and serenity. As much as possible, I use whatever is necessary to create an inviting atmosphere, one that commands habitation. The atmosphere becomes so inviting that the presence of peace can be felt upon entering. My

Preparing a Meeting Place

previous place of residence housed such a place. Upon entering the front door of my home, there was a certain spot I would lay on the floor during times of prayer. Whenever my son would come home from college to visit, he would be drawn to that area. The atmosphere was so inviting, he would sleep in my prayer spot rather than going to his room. Never mind I had just redecorated and purchased him a new mattress, which was quite comfortable. I would encourage him to go to his room, but he insisted on sleeping on the floor where I spent time communing with Father. I truly believe he was experiencing the intense peace and the angelic presence in the room.

When visitors came over, upon entering, they would automatically take their shoes off without being asked to do so. I would let them know it was okay to keep their shoes on. Nevertheless, they felt compelled to remove them. This reminded me of Moses' encounter with God at the burning bush on Mt. Sinai. Again, I believe it was the peace and the presence governing the atmosphere in the room. I also believe the same peaceful atmosphere saturated the remainder of the house as well due to the many angelic encounters and divine visitations I had with the Holy Spirit.

No matter where you find yourself, whether you have access to an entire house or only a room in a house, I encourage you to carve out part of that space as a private meeting place with Father. It will be your place purposed by design. There is no cookie cutter way to establish a meeting place. Don't make the mistake of trying to duplicate or compare your environment with someone else and their way of doing things.

Whatever is applicable to your individual style and taste, your environment will be a representation of your heart's expression. Your personality determines the furniture and props you incorporate into your sanctuary. God will help you through this process as well, if you so desire. He takes delight in the things you do for him, such as a parent should. Your desire to please Him is His delight. Keep in mind, there are no set rules. There is no right or wrong way. Therefore, whatever it takes to make your atmosphere comfortable and inviting, feel free to be creative in your expression.

> *For we live by faith, not by sight. (2 Corinthians 5:7)*

> *The spirit is willing, but the flesh is weak. (Matthew 26:41)*

The amount of time you spend in your garden is another matter. In my efforts to encourage individuals, I have heard it said numerous times, *I can't seem to concentrate and sit still that long.* I can tell you there will be times you will feel as if nothing is happening, but continue to push past those feelings and continue worshipping, meditating and praying until you break through. Your pursuit is by faith. As you develop and grow, this will no longer be an issue. Until then, start off small and gradually extend your stay each time you enter. Never measure yourself and how you spend time against someone else. This will do one or two things. It will create a sense of competitiveness or you may fall into condemnation for not being able to measure up.

Atmosphere in worship is very important. Distractions have a profound effect and will interrupt your flow. It is helpful to get away from familiar surroundings. Everything does not require money. Something as simple as taking a walk or spending time in a park appeals to some. Going away for the weekend is another idea. My favorite place of retreat is to a quiet beach. There are quite a few beaches on the coast of North Carolina, which are within a two hour driving distance. Getting up early in the morning, packing a lunch driving to the beach and returning home later in the day is an excellent get away. You avoid the cost of a hotel stay, meals and time away from work, but are still able to enjoy intimate times of worship away from the daily routine. However you choose to break away, be creative in your adventures. You will grow to appreciate these times and your desire for more will increase.

I will meditate in thy precepts, and have respect unto thy ways. (Psalm 119:15)

To meditate in Hebrew is sē'·akh, which means to consider, put forth thoughts. There is an art to meditation, and it will take some getting used to. If you are new to this concept, you may find it difficult in the beginning. It takes practice in learning how to control your thoughts and shut out the distraction of life. If you have tried and failed, I encourage you to try again. Keep trying until you become a master. It is not necessary for a person be postured in what we may consider a meditative state or position. Whether you realize it or not, everyone meditates, and we do it regularly.

Meditation is simply an act of repetitive thinking or rehearsing thoughts. Contrary to what you may have been taught, meditation is not some foreign demonic ritual or idol worship. In some cultures, yes, but meditation is an art and act of worship. Unfortunately, this form of worship has become taboo within the Christian culture. The truth is, scripture teaches us to do this consistently. We are taught to study. Study means to think deeply, reflect, or consider. This is how the human mind learns.

> *Study to shew thyself approved unto God, a workman that needeth not to be ashamed, rightly dividing the word of truth. (2 Timothy 2:15)*

Proverbs 25:2 teaches us that it is an honor to search out a matter. We are not studying for God's approval, nor are we studying for His benefit. We already have His approval and He already knows what is in the book. The purpose and goal of studying is to become aware of our inheritance and how to function as Kingdom citizens. When we study something long enough, it becomes a part of our psyche.

> *But be ye doers of the word, and not hearers only, deceiving your own selves. (James 1:22)*

It is not enough to simply read for the sake of reading. We are to read for understanding so we can apply it to our activities of daily living. One thing is certain; the word of God works when we allow it to work. However, success and victorious living will not happen by accident. The application of scripture has to be intentional. Therefore, we meditate and study for our own growth and development. God's word needs to become so ingrained that we are continually transformed as a result.

Come unto me, all you that labor and are heavy laden, and I will give you rest. (Matthew 11:28)

Soaking prayer is another phrase used to describe a position of resting in the presence of God. Unfortunately, there are those who do not agree with the use of this terminology either, but this will not be debated here. Nonetheless, I believe it is a simple play on words. Soaking prayer is the same concept as meditating. A few years ago, there was a television commercial advertising a bath product called calgon. The commercial depicted a woman soaking in a bubble bath. As she laid back to relax, she uttered the now famous phrase *calgon take me away.* The goal was to get you to believe that using this product would relieve you of all your stress as you submerge in a relaxing bath.

Meditation, thinking, soaking, submerging, relaxing are all words associated with the process of mentally, emotionally and physically resting in an atmosphere of worship. As you soak in His presence and meditate on His goodness, your heart will be comforted and relieved of life's burdens. An atmosphere cultivated by you and the Holy Spirit is like soil that has been tilled and nourished for planting. When seed is planted in good ground, a bountiful harvest is produced.

I pray this helps you to have a better understanding about the benefits of meditation and how soaking, praying, resting or whatever word you choose to use for being in a meditative atmosphere of worship can change your life. Your meeting place is a personalized sanctuary that will have your fingerprint. I encourage you to visit this place as much as possible. It will without a doubt, help you mature and develop. You will begin to see the puzzle pieces come together and understand the mysteries to the questions you have about your life.

Learning to maximize every moment and grow from every experience, even the negative ones is a process.
~ ~ ~

Memorial Stones

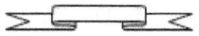

The LORD is my strength and shield. I trust him with all my heart. He helps me, and my heart is filled with joy. (Psalm 28:7 NIV)

It is a natural response to run away when we are afraid of something, or when we perceive danger is near. This is a natural human instinct called *fight or flight*. We have two choices to either stand and fight or give in to fear and follow the instinct to run. There are times we have no choice but to fight. However, standing in the midst of danger, or what we perceive to be dangerous, takes a great deal of emotional and mental courage. Depending on the situation, it may require using physical strength to overcome adversity. One thing is for sure, you never know how strong you are until all you have is courage.

> *For God hath not given us the spirit of fear; but of power, and of love, and of a sound mind. (1 Timothy 1:7)*

There are many things in life that may cause us to be afraid, but scripture teaches us not to be timid. Instead, we are to stand in the confidence of God's strength and the power of His Holy Spirit. Let's be real; this is easier said than done. Fear is a reflex. God gave us this emotion for a reason. Should we then run whenever we feel fear? If you are fleeing a situation because your life is in danger, the answer is a resounding yes! Should you run from emotional fear? I would say stand and fight because you are able to overcome these types of fears over time. This is especially true when you find yourself running to keep from dealing with heartache, loss or any type of pain stemming from situational traumas. This type of fear keeps you broken, bound, stagnated and in bondage. It is not alright to run when we use fear as an excuse not to deal with heart issues. These are the types of emotions that keep you from progressing.

> *For I know the thoughts that I think toward you, saith the LORD, thoughts of peace, and not of evil, to give you an expected end. (Jeremiah 29:11)*

The Holy Spirit will help you get to know yourself and understand why you do what you do, the way you do it. Much of how you respond is personality, while other reactions and responses are reactive or learned behaviors. Having a better understanding of the root causes of fear will help you channel and redirect how you deal with situational issues more effectively. It will require illumination and coming into agreement with the plan of God for your life. In God's presence is a place where you are able to dialogue, unravel and identify these unfortified areas. There you will gain the strength to stand against the pressures of the issues you can't seem to get past. It is possible to deal with something for so long, it becomes a part of our reality. We then no longer recognize it as being a problem.

Learning to maximize every moment and grow from every experience, even the negative ones, is a process. To begin this process of healing, you must expand and change your focus. You must also change your vision of how you see yourself. We tend to view things from personal perspectives shaped by life experiences. Everyone at one point or another has been through or will have some type of traumatic experience. These experiences can become vividly etched in the psyche. I refer to these as memorial stones. They mark places of pain and become *last time* reminders to prevent similar encounters. These are stones of emotional places that become memorialized reminders we use as road blocks, caution lights and stop signs throughout our lives. We then use these experiences to remind and guard ourselves against future painful encounters. This is a great recipe for what scripture refers to as hardening of the heart, which is a process that happens over time. It is not something most of us intentionally decide to do. It becomes a knee-jerk and mechanical reaction to protect ourselves from pain. This develops into a defense mechanism against the ability to trust.

When our hearts become numb, we refuse to allow anyone or anything to penetrate those broken and tender places. Those memorial stones become entrenched and prevent the heart from feeling. Unfortunately, this also blocks the entryway preventing healthy emotions as well. With continual exposure to painful situations, the heart (soul) becomes harder to penetrate. We become disillusioned and unconsciously govern our lives and decisions based on these negative experiences. Unfortunately, in an attempt to protect our hearts, we end up protecting the pain that cocoons our heart.

At some point we have all said the infamous *I will never*. This is an outward expression of an internal decision to guard and protect. For example, your first plane ride may not have been so pleasant for whatever reason. The experience was so traumatic you made the decision to never take another plane ride. Your heart became harden against the idea of flying. A memorial stone of fear now guards your heart and guides your decision to never fly again. There are also memorial stones you may have borrowed from another person's traumatic experience. You did not experience the plane ride personally, but based on someone else's experience, you are now afraid to fly. Does this sound familiar? For every negative experience we tend to gather these stones. We then become locked into cycles of bondage that keep us from maturing as much as we could or should. Whenever we are presented with new opportunities, ideas or challenges, we tend to look back at what I call *last time* reminders and make decisions based on their painful landmarks. So what happens in the face of emotional fear? We use the past as an excuse to run away and miss out on the promises and blessings of God. The cycle continues, as we cannot seem to break free from the patterns and fabricated beliefs that have over time become our reality.

> *I am come that they might have life, and that they might have it more abundantly. (John 10:10b)*
>
> *Jesus said unto her, I am the resurrection, and the life: he that believes in me, though he were dead, yet shall he live: (John 11:25)*

At the root of all fear is the lack of trust. Fear is keeping many of us from being in sync with Father. I have come to realize our level of trust is not where we think it is. This is evident when we are tested. We speculate or convince ourselves we are brave and have overcome, but we really do not know how we will respond until we are confronted. Unfortunately, when put to the test, we often fail. The good news is, confrontation is not a bad thing because so much is revealed in those moments of testing. These are opportunities to see just how stable we truly are versus how stable we think we are emotionally. Instead of getting upset and out of sorts during times of testing, we should use these encounters as a measuring device for growth and maturity. I believe God uses these moments to bring about exposure to identify our handicaps, crutches and unfortified places. These unsightly places are difficult to look at or revisit, which is why the heart attempts to keep them buried and protected from view. Consider this analogy of how we bury the deceased. Once we lay dead things to rest, a memorial or headstone is placed as a grave marker and identifier. Whenever you experience hurt and shut down areas of your emotions, you are placing a grave marker for yourself and a headstone that shows others *here lies death to something that once was alive*. Over time, death becomes apparent through a display of actions and responses. There is no place for dead things among the living. God's desire is for us to be fully functional in every area of life. Where there is death, there is no hope, joy or aspiration; but there is good news.

> *And I will restore to you the years that the swarming locust has eaten, the crawling locust, and the consuming locust, and the cutting locust, my great army which I sent among you. (Job 2:25)*

God is not only one who rewards, He specializes in restoring. He is able to resurrect the hopeless and lost, especially our ability to love and receive love. Let me warn you, there are no quick fixes. It will require work that can sometimes be extensive. Some stones are hidden deeper than others requiring longer hours and more persistence in order to uproot them. However, the first step in the process is complete and total surrender.

> *Hear ye therefore the parable of the sower. When any one heareth the word of the kingdom, and understandeth it not, then cometh the wicked one, and catcheth away that which was sown in his heart. This is he which received seed by the way side. But he that received the seed into stony places, the same is he that heareth the word, and anon with joy receiveth it; yet hath he not root in himself, but dureth for a while: for when tribulation or persecution ariseth because of the word, by and by he is offended. He also that received seed among the thorns is he that heareth the word; and the care of this world, and the deceitfulness of riches, choke the word, and he becometh unfruitful. But he that received seed into the good ground is he that heareth the word, and understandeth it; which also beareth fruit, and bringeth forth, some an hundredfold, some sixty, some thirty. (Matthew 13:18-23)*

Consider the parable of the sower. This is a perfect picture of the heart. The condition of the soil (heart), will determine the harvest (results) we will reap. I love plants and flowers and the way they beautify a lawn. The look and feel of a well-manicured lawn is phenomenal, but I am by no means a gardener or landscape artist. When I purchased my home, both my driveway and the road I lived on was gravel. This would later be paved with asphalt and cement. I remember wanting to plant two rows of Patriot Perennial Hosta. How hard could it be? You simply dig a hole. Then you place the plant in, cover and water it right? I thought the process would be fairly simple, but not so. Listen to how the passage unfolded. In preparing the soil, I began digging and disturbing the soil. As I dug deeper, additional layers of gravel and other types of stone were revealed. I discovered the previous house, which was on the lot before it burned down, had a driveway laid with brick. Not only did I have to dig up the top layer of gravel, I also had to remove the other layers as well. This took quite a bit of work. In order for the roots to have enough room to grow, I had to dig deeper than I had originally planned. By the time this project was finished, I ached in places where I didn't know I had muscles. When I sat back and began to ponder on the condition of the soil as it relates to the condition of our hearts, the scriptures came alive. The hardness of the soil put up a resistance to digging. It was no small undertaking. It took much work to get the soil prepared. This is what it looks like when we are not pliable and resist the work of the Holy Spirit. Then life and circumstances are tools that are used to break up the fallow ground (hard places) in our lives. To surrender is to cease resistance and submit to authority. It is not until we are in a surrendered condition and position that we are able to get in agreement with the Holy Spirit. We then are able to identify, get rid of and uproot every hard and stony place.

Looking at the condition of the soil I was working with as it related to my heart, there was much work to do. Like the Apostle Peter when he said to Jesus, *wash all of me Lord*, I was ready to surrender and allow God to purge me of everything hindering our relationship. My prayer focus became *Father, reveal to me every hidden place of resistance*. I began praying for what I call heart massages. The purpose of a massage is to get rid of all the kinks and hard places causing a particular area to be stiff. As I prayed, I envisioned the hand of God squeezing and rubbing out the rough places like a potter would do with a lump of clay. It is the same as having a deep tissue massage. The pressure is intense and it hurts. Massaging pressure is necessary pressure in order to get the muscles to relax.

I sought the LORD, and he heard me, and delivered me from all my fears. (Psalm 34:4)

I knew it would not be easy, but I was determined to work with the Holy Spirit in order to be free by any means necessary. It would take standing in the midst of what I feared the most and allowing Father to help me deal with every painful place as it was uncovered. This meant coming out of a state of denial, facing the issue(s) and acknowledging there were problems.

Denial is the illusion of truth or not admitting to what is truth. Unfortunately, not wanting to face reality also keeps us tied to our comfort zones. Everything we do is a choice and to stay in the zone of comfort is a choice. The world of psychology will explain to you, to remain in denial is a choice. It is a way to escape from reality, which boils down to being another form of defense against unbearable pain. We all have gone through some form of denial at some point or another. It is a part of the five stages of grief, which is not limited to death. Grief happens when there is a loss of any kind, such as a broken relationship, loss of a job or possessions, etc. However, ignoring something does not make it go away. You're only suppressing it. The more you suppress it, the deeper you bury it until it becomes hidden from your radar. The ugly truth is the fact that it is not really hidden. Pain is displayed in many ways, such as mood swings, withdrawal, over compensating or some other form of negative behavior. Therefore, the answer is to accept and deal with the *elephant in the room* in order to move on.

> *But God hath chosen the foolish things of the world to confound the wise; and God hath chosen the weak things of the world to confound the things which are mighty; (I Corinthians 1:27-29).*

There is a difference between going through and GROWING through. Running to or into painful situations goes against human instinct and everything we have been taught about protecting ourselves. However, God uses uncommon things to bring about great results. He has ways of doing things that we may ordinarily consider foolish, but have divine purpose. Instead of running away from fear and using them for reasons not to engage, a more effective strategy is to RUN TO the pain. Run to the thing(s) that causes you to retreat, turn away from and/or not think about because it causes your heart to flutter and your stomach to churn with fear and dread. Yes that! Don't run, give in, or back down. Stand flatfooted and deal with whatever is causing you NOT TO pursue! You are MORE THAN the sum total of your apprehensions. Apply pressure to it instead of allowing whatever it is to pressure you. This probably goes against every instinct within you or sounds quite foolish. That's the point. God never said we wouldn't hurt or have disappointment. Just know when we do, He is right there through it all. He is more than able to carry and help us heal through the pain. Remember, CHANGE is a process. You may or may not feel better in the morning. One thing is for certain. As you continue to confront emotional issues, you will gain strength to obtain what once seemed out of reach.

Surrender to the archeologist as He takes you through the process of excavation. Make the decision to work with Him to be free from every place of bondage keeping you in an arrested developmental condition. You have already overcome every enemy, generational curse and sin. Jesus took care of it all on the cross, and **ALL** these things are **FOREVER** broken off your life. You have everything you need for living a life of liberty. You are indeed a righteous heir within the Kingdom of heaven.

Excuses are the antidote to progression.
~ ~ ~

The Process of Excavation

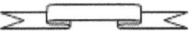

Is not my word like as a fire? saith the LORD; and like a hammer that breaketh the rock in pieces? (Jeremiah 23:29)

Excavation is a controlled exploration of what lies underneath the surface, hidden things that are systematically exposed. It is a slow and tedious process that involves digging. The process is difficult that involves penetrating and breaking through densely packed soil, rocks and stone. The purpose of the breaking is to reveal past activity that took place and became hidden over time.

The process of excavation reveals valued treasure that has been lost or hidden away. Over time, these treasures become covered by years of soil, weed, dirt and debris. Much can be learned when we discover our history.

It has been said, *time heals all wounds*. On the contrary; if not dealt with, time only hides wounds. They will eventually become hardened emotional places. As previously discussed, these memorial stony places become road blocks and blessing blockers designed to keep you from receiving what God has ordained for your life.

One of the most difficult things about teaching adults is getting them to let go of outdated information, beliefs and ways of doing things that have become nothing more than unfruitful habits. This will require a process of excavation, the digging and hollowing out to prepare and make room for something new. This process is heavily fought against because as humans, we become comfortable in our conditions. Comfort causes us to settle. When we become settled, we become stagnate and stuck. When we become stagnate and stuck, we overlook the obvious and conform for the sake of remaining comfortable. We have been taught that it's God's responsibility to do everything, which is another excuse and a way of escape. If you do not like the position or condition you are in, the responsibility to change begins and ends with you. Change is a posture and condition of the mind, which begins with a decision. We pray for change, but do we really mean it? Change requires movement. Oftentimes, what was once good and familiar can become baggage at the point of transition and there will be no room for it in the new place. There comes a time when we have to unpack (spiritually, emotionally and physically) to make room for the new. Change is not always easy, but it is necessary. However, we allow fear to keep us in a state of arrested development. We cannot continue to allow fear of something new to keep us from embracing the place of growth, freedom, liberty and purpose God is calling us to occupy.

As the process of evaluation is taking place, it is imperative for us to change our focus. Otherwise, we will halt the plan and purpose of the process. Changing your focus and how you look at your condition empowers you to make better decisions. Changing your focus helps alleviate the dread of having to do things you might consider unpleasant. Begin to look at DOING as an opportunity. This will diminish the mental stress and emotional pressures that come with HAVING TO. For example, I have to go to work. No, rather look at it as I get to go to work, because I am thankful to have a job. This allows me to pay my bills and have nice things. I have to exercise. No, rather than thinking of it as forcible habit, think of it as an opportunity to do something that will make life enjoyable. For instance, I get to exercise because I want to feel better, stay in good health and look nice in my clothes. I have to stay in this relationship. No, I get to stay because I want this relationship, marriage, or partnership to be all I saw it could be from the beginning. I have to read, study and pray. No, I get to do these things because I desire to know who I am from God's perspective; I get to understand my inheritance and walk in the fullness of my kingdom citizenship. We've all been there. In order for me to do this or have this, I have to do that. Complaining about your have to moments never solves anything. It is an ingredient for frustration, temper tantrums and pity parties. Understand this beloved; you will never be forced to be happy, to be better, or to be prosperous. You don't have to do anything you don't want to do. Your choices have and always will be yours to make. By changing your focus from the **HAVE TO** dreads into I **GET TO** opportunities, there will be notable differences in your life. When you do this on a regular basis, you will discover its positive impact on your energy levels, motivational drive, health, and your overall quality of life will change for the better.

Excuses are the antidote to progression. Have you noticed what happens when someone is resistant to change? To keep from shifting, changing or transitioning they will use any excuse or find a reason to blame someone else for why they cannot, should not or will not. I am reminded of a certain man in scripture who had become comfortable in his condition of being crippled.

> *Now a certain man was there who had an infirmity thirty-eight years. When Jesus saw him lying there, and knew that he already had been in that condition a long time, He said to him, "Do you want to be made well?" The sick man answered Him, "Sir, I have no man to put me into the pool when the water is stirred up; but while I am coming, another steps down before me." Jesus said to him, "Rise, take up your bed and walk." And immediately the man was made well, took up his bed, and walked. (John 5:5-9)*

When Jesus asked him if he wanted to change his condition, notice he immediately began making excuses and blaming others. This is a behavior that goes back to the garden. Adam blamed God first and then Eve for being banned from Eden.

> *And the man said, the woman whom thou gavest to be with me, she gave me of the tree, and I did eat. (Genesis 3:12).*

He blamed God for giving him the woman. Then he blamed Eve because she gave him the fruit. How often have we blamed God for our invalid conditions? It happens more than we are willing to admit. In order to change, there are two options; continue blaming and complaining, or deal with your situation by getting up and doing something about it. This certain man had been lying there complaining and blaming for thirty-eight years. Then Jesus comes along and challenges his mindset. Jesus had the audacity to hold the man accountable by telling him to get up. Jesus did not lay hands or wave some magic wand over him. He simply challenged his condition. Every now and again there will be someone or something that will come to challenge you. This is to push you beyond your current mental and sometimes physical limitations. This man probably thought to himself, if this Jesus has enough confidence and believes I am able to walk, the least I can do is try. Take notice what happened to the man. He made the decision he no longer wanted to be crippled. IMMEDIATELY, his situation changed. He decided to believe for the better. He decided to put his faith into action and make a change. He decided he would no longer wait on someone else to hold his hand or BLAME them for his condition. It was up to him to do something about his situation. The miracle did not happen when this certain man got up and began walking. The miracle happened when he changed his mind and decided he could walk. Then he got up. EVERYTHING we do; everything we say and everything we are or ever will be begins with a decision.

Now faith is the substance of things hoped for, the evidence of things not seen. (Hebrews 11:1)

The word NOW is very important because now means immediately or in the moment. You must first see yourself being what you believe you are before it manifests. It's called faith. In other words, don't believe because you see it, see it because you believe. Allow your actions to speak to your belief in God. Life will challenge you, but the Holy Spirit will guide you beyond your mental and physical limitations. Here again, it will not be easy, but it will be well worth it. Unfortunately, like the certain lame man in John 5:5-9, until the pain of staying the same becomes greater than the pain to change, you won't! Therefore, your desire for what you want to do has to be more powerful than your current comfort.

For years, Father would emphasize His desire by telling me, *I'm trying to get some things to you.* Each time, I would hear it I would become puzzled. Then I would become frustrated because I thought it was a simple matter of God just giving me whatever it was He wanted me to have. In many Christian doctrines, we are taught to view God like Santa Claus having the responsibility of blessing us with toys and making our lives happy. So, what was the problem? I was speaking, seeking, confessing, reading my Bible, praying, going to church, ministering and doing all the right things; so I thought. However, it wasn't that simple. It was not until I met God in the secret place that He began sharing with me and unfolding the secret places of my heart. It was there I discovered it was mental fears and emotional strongholds keeping me locked into a crippled condition.

Everyone has a story and here is just a small piece of my testimony. My biggest stronghold like so many others was one of trust. I remember one Saturday afternoon during the month of June 2007. I was lying across my couch when I began having an open vision of God's hand holding a heart. It was not a red valentine heart like the ones we cut out of construction paper as children. This was a beating, beautifully pink, brand new human heart that appeared to be very soft and fragile. I instinctively knew this heart was quite tender and sensitive. It looked as if anyone were to touch this heart it would stop beating and die. I know this may sound dramatic, but these were my thoughts, which unconsciously, had become my reality. Through this vision, Like the lame man, God was showing me how emotionally broken and guarded I had become.

As the Holy Spirit continued explaining the purpose for the vision, He allowed me to know, this was a secret place. It was the part of me I had kept hidden and did not want or allow anyone to have access. He reassured me that in His hands, my heart was safe. However, there was a problem and that was, I didn't trust Him to keep it. Of course, this did not intellectually make sense to me, because if I didn't trust Him with it, why then would I give it to Him? Another thing I love about the Holy Spirit is that He has a way of teaching that infants are able to understand. He began showing where I had trust issues and why. The problem was me being afraid of exposure. He told me, you do not trust me to unveil your heart to another. At that moment, I began having chest pain and became very nauseated. I experienced the adrenaline rush of fight or flight. I immediately protested. In my heart I was screaming, *no God, you can't do that. You can't show my heart to anyone. If they see it, they will kill me.* He said, *you see daughter, you don't trust me.* As hurtful as it was, it was something I needed to recognize.

He began ministering to me about relationships and allowing myself to become vulnerable enough to receive love. As He continued to speak, the physical pain and feelings of dread continued to overwhelm me to the point I heard myself say *I'm sorry God, I can't take that chance.* It became very apparent at that point, "Houston, we have a problem." I began weeping and wrestling within myself to understand what had just happened. Like the certain man in scripture, the Holy Spirit had come to challenge my condition. God helped me to realize, not even He could penetrate and heal places of pain without having permission. Therefore, the process of excavation was necessary if we were to grow any closer.

Periodically, I would have excavation encounters with the Holy Spirit concerning my heart. Each time, I would feel a nauseating dread and fear. With each encounter, the intensity of the pain was steadily decreasing. Keep in mind, this was an area in my heart I had laid to rest and marked it with an *"I Will Never"* memorialized place of pain beginning in 1982. It was then my heart was severely broken and wounded to the point of severe depression. At that point physical death did not seem so bad. Imagine a land marked sign that reads "Danger, Do Not Enter". The stronghold of distrust was being fortified and I believe this is when a stronghold became anchored to my soul. This meant the process of uprooting and excavating would take some time.

The question still remained, what was I doing to hinder God's hand of blessing? It was not until a few years ago, I finally let go of my apprehensions long enough to see and understand what He had been trying to get me to see. Being blind and not able to see resulted from years of hiding, rejecting the truth and making excuses. My crippled condition had become my reality and what was normal had now become abnormal. Due to a wounded soul, I convinced myself love was not real; it was all a facade. I believed those who displayed affection were simply putting on an act and pretending. The mind is a powerful thing, which is why we are taught in Isaiah 26:3 to focus our thoughts on God and He will keep our minds in perfect peace.

My issue was not the ability to show and receive love. I only allowed my affections of love to be subjective and limited to family and friends. When it came to the idea of being in love, my soul became grieved. Around my heart was an engraved titanium steel grave marker that read *KEEP OUT.* In other words, *your love is not welcome here.* It was a place I had laid to rest and vowed with an *"I will never."* This was one of those *last time* reminders; a headstone that marked a burial place. Imagine a titanium steel door kept under bolted lock and key that would forever be closed to keep out pain and anyone who might inflict pain. As stated earlier, these markers were used to identify a place of death where there was once life.

> *Jesus said unto her, I am the resurrection, and the life: he that believes in me, though he were dead, yet shall he live: (John 11:25)*

God is a life-giving and resurrecting Spirit. He wants us to live and prosper in every area of life. My attempt at protecting myself and keeping people out was also a failed attempt at allowing God in. Not only was I blocking out human affection, I was also keeping God at bay by not allowing Him to touch, reveal and heal those intimate places. I had become accustomed to guarding places of pain. I became blind and could not see how I was blocking the Holy Spirit from healing my life. God loves us, but what we fail to realize is His love is dispensed through people. That's why scripture teaches us to love one another. When we block people out, we are also blocking the hand of God from functioning through people. We consistently reject them and remain barren, blind, weak and insensitive in condition.

Hope deferred makes the heart sick: but when the desire is fulfilled, it is a tree of life. (Proverbs 13:12)

The rejected often becomes the rejecter. You see this behavior so much in children who are in foster care. Rather than continually have their hearts broken and affections rejected, it is easier not to hope at all. They often act out these emotions by throwing temper tantrums, running away and getting into trouble. Experiencing repeated disappointment triggers this defense mechanism in both children and adults. As adults, we also tend to throw temper tantrums and run away to keep from experiencing the trauma of having our hearts repeatedly broken. This had become my rationale. Although wounded and blind, I still loved the idea of loving, giving and sharing as long as I was the one doing the giving. I would be the one in control of affections; the operative word being *control*.

> *There is a way which seems right unto a man, but the end thereof are the ways of death. (Proverbs 14:12)*

Opening your heart and allowing someone to occupy an emotional place is a state of becoming intimate and vulnerable. It requires letting your defenses down. It is easy to give up, but it requires faith and strength to trust. My defense mechanism was to play *keep away*. By doing so, I would avoid the pain of losing something precious to me, such as love. My heart was too fragile, and the risk of another emotional devastation was too great. This is what I meant when I told God I was not willing to take that chance.

Many of God's children are suffering from the *foster child* syndrome. We remain closed and reject Him out of fear of being rejected. Imagine trying to get something through a closed door. You can't. God needs open access and permission into every area of our lives. Until those areas are excavated and refortified, we will continue to run away and reject God's hand of blessing.

> *Beloved, I wish above all things that you may prosper and be in health, even as your soul prospers. (3 John 1:2)*

God desires to prosper us in every area of life. He knows what we need better than we know ourselves. The thing He is trying to get to many of us, the thing we keep rejecting is His unconditional LOVE. God is not like man *(Numbers 23:19)*. His love is without limits. It is not based on our behavior or what we consider good. He will never take His love from us. God is love *(1 John 4:8)*. By preventing love, we prevent him. The intimacy we so desperately seek is the very thing many of us reject. This is a result of being fragmented.

> *Arise, and go down to the potter's house, and there I will cause thee to hear my words. Then I went down to the potter's house, and, behold, he wrought a work on the wheels. And the vessel that he made of clay was marred in the hand of the potter: so he made it again another vessel, as seemed good to the potter to make it. (Jeremiah 18:2-4)*

Post-traumatic stress is a condition that develops after a person is exposed to a traumatic event. A loss of any kind can be devastating; after which we become broken, fragile and fragmented. There is a disconnection happening between the intellect and the emotions. Mentally we feel ready to conquer the world, but emotionally we remain weak and vulnerable. This is an internal warfare many of us fail to recognize. I am reminded of the potters' wheel and how He takes a broken vessel and repairs it to look new again. God is that potter, who has the wisdom and skill to put us back together again. We simply need to stay seated on the wheel in His presence and allow Him to work.

> *Can two walk together, except they be agreed? (Amos 3:3)*

Despite what is taught, the Holy Spirit is a gentleman and will never invade places and spaces where He is not allowed. He enters by invitation only. Therefore, our emotional desire and intellectual desire must be in agreement for access to be granted.

> *And be not conformed to this world: but be ye transformed by the renewing of your mind, that ye may prove what is that good, and acceptable, and perfect, will of God. (Romans 12:2)*

In the chapter Knowing God as Father, I made reference to deliverance. Deliverance is a process and it has been taught in the church that the process involves casting out demons. I will not negate there are times when we have to deal with demonic entities, but it is not always necessary to have someone lay hands and call out evil spirits in order to receive deliverance. Much of what has been called demonic is nothing more than stubborn mindsets and old thought processes. Thoughts and mindsets, by the way, cannot be cast out. The mind has to be transformed and renewed. This is not to say deliverance is not necessary. Jesus proved the need for deliverance through His death on the cross and by doing so said *it is finished*. Once we come to understand and accept the finished work of the cross, the need to be delivered from demons will be less important or necessary.

> *Now there are diversities of gifts, but the same Spirit. And there are differences of administrations, but the same Lord. And there are diversities of operations, but it is the same God which worketh all in all. But the manifestation of the Spirit is given to every man to profit withal. (1 Corinthians 12:4-7)*

We make the mistake of becoming fixated on one way of doing things. Doctrine and ministries are birthed from movements that were only meant to be administrative parts of and not the sum total of what we often call ministry. The Bible teaches there are diverse administrations of the same gift, but God is the one who works through them all. As it relates to being set free, expelling demons is not the only method of deliverance.

> *Come to me, all you that labor and are heavy laden, and I will give you rest. (Matthew 11:28)*
>
> *Cast your burden on the LORD, and he shall sustain you: he shall never suffer the righteous to be moved. (Psalm 55:22)*

When you get in agreement with Father and what His word says concerning your situation, deliverance takes place. I believe in the power of agreement. When you are resting in the Garden of God's presence during times of intimate worship, your heart is laid bare. He will show you the hard places that need to be weeded, uprooted and eliminated from the garden of your heart. It is at this point you must decide to get in agreement with the Holy Spirit and accept what He is showing you so the process of excavation can begin. Once there, you will enter into a place of deliverance and rest. Sometimes, the process is immediate, while at other times, the process is longer. How much time it takes is determined by your willingness to go through the process. This is a proven method in my life and the lives of countless others I have trained and mentored.

weeping may stay for the night, but rejoicing comes in the morning. (Psalm 30:5b)

There will be times when it seems unbearable, but don't be moved by what you see, hear or feel. At some point in our maturation process we must learn to stand and embrace pain instead of running from it. You will have to fight, but the fight is one of faith (1 Timothy 6:12). This will begin once you determine you are ready for change and willing to do whatever it takes to make CHANGE happen. Therefore, fight against the pain of staying the same. Wage war against past offenses. Stand your ground. Fight against those memorial reminders that come to steal and cause you to retreat. Cry when you have to, scream if you must, but hang in there and endure the process. Once excavation is accomplished, the stony places of your heart become flesh again. The crooked places in your heart are made straight, allowing you to become more aware. Learning (planting), adapting to (repositioning) and applying the new (correct) information becomes easier. The end of a thing is sometimes greater than the beginning. Stay the course. God is trying to get some things to you. Don't fight the process.

**The answers to everything you need is
In the Garden of His Presence**
~ ~ ~

Final Thoughts

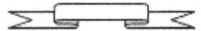

But the fruit of the Spirit is love, joy, peace, longsuffering, gentleness, goodness, faith, Meekness, temperance: against such there is no law. (Galatians 5:22-23)

In the beginning, the Garden was given to mankind to sustain them. Everything they needed was within their reach. God *prepared a meeting place* where they would commune with Him daily. Imagine it, living life with daily walks and talks with God. Have you ever thought to yourself, there has to be *more than this?* I can emphatically tell you yes. There is more. You may even find yourself asking God for more of Him. Beloved, you do not need more of God. You have as much of Him as you will ever have. What you need is a greater revelation of what has already been provided and given to you. As you become more comfortable in *knowing God as Father*, you will excel in learning how to receive from the realm of son-ship. As a son you do not need permission. You have been given free access and will find everything you need in the garden of His presence. It is there He will inform, instruct and guide you through life's situations. Making Him a priority should not be an option, it should be your reality. Set aside time and spend a few *date nights* with Him just as you would a significant other. During such intimate times, your relational development will be enhanced quite significantly. No time spent with Father is ever insignificant.

Scripture teaches us in Romans 12:2 to be in the world, but do not conform to the ways of this world. Life will indeed happen, but when you focus on your problems more than you focus on God, this is an indication you have been away from the Garden too long. When you find yourself frustrated, angry, lonely, dealing with or displaying anything other than the fruit of God's Spirit, you have strayed away from the Garden. These are also signs there could be *memorial stones* needing to be uprooted so growth can take place in those areas of your life. He is well able to strengthen you through the *process of excavation* and restore what has been lost. When you find

Final Thoughts

yourself in situations contrary to scripture or acting opposite to who God says you are; ask yourself, when was the last time I visited the Garden? It is essential for us to have a healthy diet to feed our natural bodies. It is also essential that we partake of the Garden and be strengthened in order to remain full of the peace, joy, faith and goodness it provides. When we are absent from the table of God, we run the risk of being filled with other things.

> *for the LORD your God goes with you; he will never leave you nor forsake you. (Deuteronomy 31:6)*

God is faithful even when we are not. He never fails. No matter how long we've strayed away, He will never turn us away in our pursuit of Him. No matter what burdens you carry, how undeserving you may feel, God is greater than all of them. What concerns you, concerns Him. No problem is too big or too small. He is always available with open arms to welcome you. You are His beloved, the apple of His eye. When the issues of life seem to become unbearable, always remember, the answer to everything you need is found in *the garden of His presence.*

> *I pray that the eyes of your heart may be enlightened in order that you may know the hope to which he has called you, the riches of his glorious inheritance in his holy people, and his incomparably great power for us who believe according to the working of His mighty power (Ephesians 1:18-19)*

It is my hope that you come to know God in an ever increasing measure. My desire is the same as Paul's pray was for the Ephesians, that you come to know Him better.

> *For there is nothing hidden that will not be disclosed, and nothing concealed that will not be known or brought out into the open. Therefore consider carefully how you listen. Whoever has will be given more; (Luke 8:17-18a)*

Art is meant to be seen and God wants to put you on display. You are His treasured work of beauty with gifts and talents on the inside of you. However, before that great reveal, there is work that needs to be done in the secret place. I bless you with peace as you abide and receive rest in the Garden of His Presence.

PRAYER

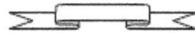

Heavenly Father,

Thank you for accepting and giving me the privilege to come and rest in your presence without fear or doubt. Because of your heart towards me, I am able to sit and learn with you. Your word teaches me, those who hunger and thirst after righteousness shall be filled. I can think of nothing or no one more righteous than you and your shed blood. It is because of your righteous act of eternal kindness that I have been accepted and made right with you. I believe neither death nor life or anything in between is able to separate me from your love.

You said If I abide in you and your word abide in me, I can ask for what I desire, and it will be done for me. Therefore, I pray for an increased awareness of any thing keeping me from entering into greater levels of intimacy with you. Reveal to me every place of pain and every hidden thing holding me emotionally hostage. My desire is to be completely free to love you with my whole heart beyond all fear and apprehension.

My goal is to make every effort to spend more time in your presence and learn of you, from you and with you. I thank you now for the gentle reminders you send to remind me when I have strayed away for too long. I believe the results of our time together will cause a greater harvest to manifest in every area as I seek to know your thoughts that will guide me into the expected end you have ordained for my life.

Amen

About the Author

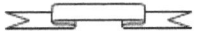

Veronica, which in Latin means True Image of Christ, is purposely driven to stir up righteous hunger in the hearts of men and women; thereby, transforming lives into passionate and relational pursuit with God. Fully committed while tenaciously pursuing the heart of God, she boldly proclaims the Gospel of Jesus Christ, sharing His love and compassion with ALL people. The impact of God's love in her life enables her to effectively live as one thoroughly understanding the need for intimacy.

> Matthew 6:19-21, "Do not lay up for yourselves treasures on earth, where moth and rust destroy and where thieves break in and steal; but lay up for yourselves treasures in heaven, where neither moth nor rust destroys and where thieves do not

break in and steal. For where your treasure is, there your heart will be also."

In meeting Veronica, you will shortly thereafter come to understand her heart's treasure is hidden in heaven which explains her desire to see individuals not only develop, but enjoy a close, personal and intimate relationship with Father God!

Believing whatever you do, you should be a specialist at it; Veronica holds a Master of Education degree in Training & Development from North Carolina State University, as well as a Bachelor of Arts degree in Public Administration from Shaw University. She often states that training is a part of her DNA and believes everyone is born with a purpose. Unfortunately, there are many who never realize that purpose. Therefore, she is a motivator who encourages individuals to pursue their dreams until those dreams become reality.

On occasion it takes another individual to help us see what we may not see in ourselves. Veronica is known for her ability to ignite enthusiasm while motivating others who simply need direction, insight or that extra push toward accomplishing their goals. Such keen insight allows her to empower both young and old to uncover hidden talent, discover additional abilities and develop untapped potential within themselves.

In her role as a Trainer, Motivational Speaker, Life Coach and Ordained Minister, she is known for her tenacious "Making Life Happen" leadership style. Her unique approach has been instrumental in assisting individuals and ministry leaders alike in areas of personal, professional and leadership growth and development.

It is through the knowledge of Jesus Christ that gives us the power to live a balanced and victorious life. Although Veronica is a multifaceted trainer, her first love is motivating individuals to develop deeper levels of intimacy in their relationship with God. She is available for all types of training events and speaking engagements upon request.

Additional Resource

There is purpose for your life. Your journey is personal and specifically designed with a distinct plan from heaven. There is so much more that you have yet to discover. It is always good to know about God, but how much more beneficial would it be to experience Him? His thoughts about you are good and very intentional. Therefore, your time with Him must also be intentional. There are precious treasures waiting to be discovered that are hidden in Father's heart. During your intimate times of fellowship you will be awakened to His desires and plan for your life.

Awaiting you in this 31 day devotional prayer journal are articles of encouragement and prayers of agreement for life and situations we all face. Veronica co-authors this journal with you as she shares some of her experiences and lessons learned along the way. If journaling is something new to you, this is an excellent resource to help you begin. If you journal regularly this is an additional tool designed to encourage you on your journey.

The answers to everything you need can be found in the Garden of His Presence.

.

For more information or to schedule Veronica for your next conference, seminar, workshop, or training event, please visit:

www.veronicaburnette.com

or

www.trueimageofchrist.org

Copyright © 2016 – by Veronica G. Burnette
All Rights Reserved

www.ingramcontent.com/pod-product-compliance
Lightning Source LLC
Chambersburg PA
CBHW071705040426
42446CB00011B/1929